A Very Special Gift For You

For:

From:

Norwood is a beautiful writer with the ability to convey volumes in the description of a simple moment.

— NAPRA Book Review

THE VISION
OF THE

Wealthy Soul™

by DR. MICHAEL R. NORWOOD

GLOBAL PUBLISHING

Norwood, Michael R.
    The vision of the wealthy soul / author: Michael R.
Norwood ; editor: Colleen Goidel ; book designer: Rudy
Ramos. — 1st ed.
    p. cm. — (The wealthy soul series)
    LCCN 2001-095338
    ISBN 0-911649-050

    1. Success. 2. Spiritual life. 1. Title.

BJ1611.2.N67 2001   158.1
                    QB101-701095

Wealthy Soul Books & Movies
Phone: 520-921-0534
Fax: 206-339-6420
E-mail: *publisher@wealthysoul.com*

STUDY GUIDE

This is a little book. It's easy and quick to read. Don't confuse its size or the simplicity of its message with the profundity of what it can do for you.

Though you can read any of the Wealthy Soul handbooks in just a few hours, they are designed to be read over and over again, one at a time, before you go to bed, when you arise, and as a reminder during the day. Don't stop until the concepts are second nature, until you traverse some of your own great challenges with them ... *until these lessons are ingrained as part of who you are ...*

a Wealthy Soul.

Introducing ...

Skeptic Al™

(our interviewer)

What, first may I ask, is a Wealthy Soul?
Are we talking about material
wealth here?

There are many materially wealthy people who are not Wealthy Souls. These people have never had a true Vision. And without a Vision, if a person is materially wealthy but not a Wealthy Soul, though they may be a good person, they might be what we humorously refer to as "S.O.B."

You mean Sons of ... ?

Absolutely not. As I said, most wealthy people are good people. On their deepest levels, they really want to contribute, want to help others, want to do higher work and have meaningful lives that touch more people. We all want this.

But in our culture, material wealth has become such a priority, those who achieve it sometimes do so by being:

Stuck On Bottom

*Stuck On Bottom? Most rich people
seem on top.*

Only from a material perspective, which does not make a Wealthy Soul. A good percentage of people in our culture – rich and otherwise – have become stuck on bottom, meaning stuck on the *bottom line.*

When a person is always focused on the bottom line, he never receives the Vision to rise to the top.

*C'mon, to survive in our world, you have to be
mindful of the bottom line.*

Of course. And Wealthy Soul's *are* mindful of the bottom line.
They're very adapted to 21st century life; they're not in denial of
the material necessities of it. They're just not *stuck* on that level –
stuck on the bottom line – to the detriment of so many other
things in their lives.

And it's surprising just how many people are stuck there,
their pursuit of success overriding their balance in life. It's a flaw
not only of materially wealthy people but of so many others in
our culture. In fact, once a person achieves material wealth, they
often relax and their higher nature does shine through. It's the
perceived "fight" on the way up, the "struggle" for a daily living
that puts people into this *bottom-line* mode.

It's to the point where the *me, myself and I* attitude is often
accepted as the way to be, leaving people at all levels of income
wondering why they feel so *un-wealthy*.

But then there are the rare few who have *Vision*.

Vision allows us to achieve the bottom line — material success — and at the same time rise to the top, achieving great spiritual wealth, as well.

Oprah Winfrey

One of the most materially wealthy women in America is Oprah Winfrey. Not an evangelist, a guru or a politician, she is one of the most spiritually influential woman in the nation.

After Oprah aired a show on yoga in April 2001, the number of Americans taking up yoga reportedly doubled. After she shared the coaching methods that enabled her to finally win her battle with obesity, millions of women lost weight and became empowered along with her. Each month, when Oprah reveals a new book that has touched her soul, it becomes an instant bestseller. After she proposed the National Child Protection Act to the U.S. Senate in 1991, it was signed into law.

Oprah's spirituality is down-to-earth and practical – the type that embraces self-development and self-empowerment. Her Vision is rooted in the powerlessness of her childhood, when she was sexually abused by family members and acquaintances. But after entering her late teens, nothing stopped her. She became a television news co-anchor at age 18, co-host of a morning talk show at age 23, and host of A.M. Chicago at age 30. Within a year came the nationally syndicated *The Oprah Winfrey Show*, which has remained television's number-one-rated talk show for 15 years.

Oprah defied every rule in the book. She was not white or male. Her beauty comes from something much more powerful and enduring. Her groundbreaking honesty about her own weight and personal struggles immediately crossed racial and gender lines, endearing her to audiences everywhere. Rather than an objective interviewer, she was an affected human being who let her viewers know that they were OK, too; more – not less – powerful because of their noble struggles.

Even with her mega-fame, power and wealth, our vision of Oprah Winfrey is that she's one of us. And the greatest power of her Vision is that by opening her own heart to hundreds of millions of viewers, she has opened our hearts to ourselves and to others.

The greatest
of Visions
touches something
universal in all
of us.

Peggy Claude-Pierre

In the early 1990's, life turned from bad to worse for Peggy Claude-Pierre. Recently divorced, Peggy's 15-year-old daughter's weight suddenly dropped from 108 pounds to 80 pounds. Her daughter, Kirsten, was suffering from anorexia nervosa, a disease in which mainly young girls starve themselves to death.

Working on her PhD in psychology, Peggy intuitively recognized that the medical approach of treating this disorder purely physiologically – which usually resulted in death – would not work for her daughter, either. Through round-the-clock love and praise, in three months the two had beat the negative voices in Kirsten's head – the voices that cause most anorexics to unconsciously commit suicide. Kirsten was permanently cured of this fatal disease.

However disaster soon struck again. Peggy's other daughter, 13-year-old Nicole, became a victum of anorexia, as well. Doctors told Peggy that Nicole would be a statistic within months. This time it took a full year of exhausting round-the-clock attention and love until Peggy saw the first signs she was defeating this deadly siege. Her daughter began smiling again.

News of Peggy's successes spread. She began receiving calls from around the world from both curious doctors and anguished parents. She began taking patients into her home, eventually having to move into a much larger home. Patients flocked to her clinic from around the world. She and her new husband went into great debt to keep the fledgling clinic afloat.

Today, the legacy of Peggy Claude-Pierre's Vision has saved hundreds of lives and created a new model of using unconditional love to triumph over a seemingly insurmountable disease.

Vision doesn't usually come like a lightening bolt. Rather, it comes as a slow crystallization of life challenges that we one day recognize as a beautiful diamond with great value to ourselves and others.

So what is Vision and how does it relate to a Wealthy Soul?

First let's talk about what makes a Wealthy Soul*. A Wealthy Soul is any man or woman who triumphs over great life challenges to find the finest states of spiritual and often material sustenance.

We all must face our own challenges and they recur constantly throughout our lifetime. Such challenges focus us. Though often not readily apparent, they provide opportunities for growth that may be otherwise unavailable.

When people try to avoid adversity or run away from others who are facing challenges, whatever wealth they believe they have is truly an illusion because it can be snatched away from them in an instance.

---

* See *The Path of the Wealthy Soul* by Dr. Michael R. Norwood.

Adversity provides a foundation for a wealth that can never be taken from us.

So adversity is inherent
in becoming a Wealthy Soul?

Yes. Particularly major adversity.

The greater the adversity, the more profound the wealth.

Mother Teresa

Mother Teresa, perhaps the greatest Wealthy Soul of the 20th century, didn't go to Beverly Hills to find her wealth. She went to Calcutta, India to work, in her own words, with "the dying, the crippled, the mentally ill, the unwanted and the unloved."

Unlike many of us, Mother Teresa didn't shun adversity – she embraced it. She recognized it as the sacred millstone that unearths what is most holy and most beautiful in every human being.

Such was Mother Teresa's contribution to dignifying and uplifting the ravished individuals she touched – people whose adversities make most of what we, in western civilization, face, pale in comparison – she inspired the entire world with her strength and selflessness. In fact, she can hardly be described as a Wealthy Soul, at all. "A rare, living saint" were the words commonly used to portray her before her death in 1997.

For Mother Teresa, adversity laid her bare, uncovered a deeper nature, and opened her soul to something much Bigger and Higher than herself. It does the same for us.

The pain and adversity we face in our culture is as real to us as that faced in any other. Whether our challenges involve illness, separation, money or loss, Mother Teresa's understanding applies equally to our lives:

Overcoming adversity bestows a power that leads to great spiritual wealth … and potential material wealth, as well.

Bill Warner

Bill Warner is founder of *Avid Technology*, a half-billion dollar corporation. His company sells technology that dramatically speeds the film editing process.

To begin with nothing, develop a brand new technology, have the strength and conviction to create a hugely successful enterprise of it – and win an Oscar for Technical Merit to boot – requires incredible resilience of character.

The fact that Bill Warner has had almost no use of his legs his entire adult life makes this achievement even more remarkable. A car accident when he was a teenager created that obstacle. It also helped create that resilience.

"The lesson," he says on a CNN interview, "is to embrace your life, what happens to you, where it takes you and not to fight it."

Bill Warner certainly seems to know how to find that life flow. He is currently building several other companies around other innovative technologies he's developed. One, called *Wildfire* – a phone system with an electronic personal assistant that screens and forwards calls and organizes phone messages – has already been sold to a British telecommunications firm.

One of Bill Warner's favorite projects is mentoring budding entrepreneurs, helping them learn the skills necessary to achieve their dreams, despite any adversity they may face.

It is during our times of greatest challenges that we receive our most profound revelations – and our clearest Vision.

So, what is Vision?

Some call it *The Mission*, some *The Goal*, and others *The Dream*. Though these play a role in its fruition, they don't begin to capture the sheer power and exquisiteness of a man with a *Vision*.

No man is more powerful than one with a Vision.

Wonderful. So we now know what Vision isn't.
Can you give us a little hint what it is?

Vision can best be explained in context to *The 9 Insights of the Wealthy Soul*♦ – the stages of transformation that a Wealthy Soul can consciously and attentively follow, step by step, to achieve anything desired in life: peace, balance, a goal, a dream, material wealth, happiness, etc.

Insight itself is the first insight. This powerful event occurs when one sees beyond the surface of something to perceive a much deeper value. Insight leads to discovery, revelation, love and, ultimately, a sense of oneness.

♦ See *The 9 Insights of the Wealthy Soul* by Dr. Michael R. Norwood.

Vision, in its most profound form, is the first of the 9 Insights.

Sounds important.

It is. It revolutionizes the Wealthy Soul's life.

When Mother Theresa went to Calcutta, her Vision was to find the embodiment of God in the most downtrodden of humanity, and help others find it in themselves. In so doing, she touched the world, became a spiritual symbol, and helped us understand the deepest nature of what makes a soul truly wealthy.

Mother Teresa's Vision was her *raison de etre*. Her *reason for being*. To become a Wealthy Soul, ours can be no less.

Vision is the Wealthy Soul's Lasting Purpose.

And Lasting Purpose is...?

Lasting Purpose is something that never dies. It lasts the lifetime of the Wealthy Soul. It empowers every moment of his hours. It is so big, no obstacle can block it; so worthy, no mistake – however dire – can sway him from it; so grand, no delay can diminish its intensity.

*Lasting Purpose,
the bearer of
Vision,
is timeless.*

Which leads us back to the question:
What is Vision?

A Vision has many components. It may start off as a goal, a mission or even a dream.

However, whereas the goal, mission, and dream describe something you accomplish ...

A Vision
is something you
become.

Yes, so you become *it. Great.*
I still don't have a clue.

The mission statement of someone who owns a bread company might be to serve the highest quality bread at the most reasonable prices to the greatest number of people. A business person's *goal* might be to become a millionaire in seven years and a multi-millionaire in nine. And an opera singer's *dream* might be to sing in Carnegie Hall.

But none of these ideals captures the grace and Lasting Purpose of a person with *a Vision.*

A Vision requires
a lifetime.

OK. That seems very profound. But isn't a lifetime a long time to wait for anything?

A Vision teaches incredible patience. It *cultures* patience. The reason is that, unlike a *goal* or a *dream* ...

*The Wealthy Soul
with a Vision has
no time pressure.*

Patience … yes, that's a good thing. But … it still doesn't answer the question: "What is it?"

A Vision is the alpha and omega of the Wealthy Soul's existence. For sure, it takes a lifetime to realize, but …

It's what gives meaning to every moment of the Wealthy Soul's existence.

Every moment? C'mon.
Is anything really that powerful?

Indeed. A man or woman with a Vision is one whose every step is counted. This is the wonder of what a Vision does. No matter how many obstacles lie in his path, a Wealthy Soul knows it will take a lifetime to achieve his Vision anyway.

Martin Luther King & Mahatma Ghandi

When MLK said the immortal words, *"I have a dream ..."* he was, in fact, saying he had a *Vision*. It was the same Vision of the founding fathers of the United States when they stated in the Declaration of Independence that *all men are created equal.*

MLK's Vision to bring that equality to African Americans began as a young boy when he was told he could no longer play with two friends because they were white and he was black. He decided to become a minister so that he could reach the largest number of people possible. On his way to earning a doctorate, he became fascinated by the nonviolent means which Mahatma Ghandi – another great Wealthy Soul with God-given Vision – had earned independence for India after nearly a century of British rule.

Neither man would ever see his Vision of racial equality and harmony come to fruition, both their lives tragically cut short by assassins. But long after their deaths, the Visions of these men continue to move not just their own people, but people of the entire world.

A Vision makes it simpler for the Wealthy Soul to surmount all obstacles, no matter how enduring.

*How can a Vision—whatever you're finally going
to say a Vision exactly is—do all that?*

Let's say a man is walking down a path and suddenly a huge boulder blocks his way. If the man stops and contemplates his bad luck, he won't get very far. Around the next bend there's always going to be another boulder. And another. And another ...

A Vision keeps the Wealthy Soul focused on the path and not on the boulders.

*Beautiful. Very philosophical. Almost touching.
Can't you give me something more practical?*

Let's look at the stock market. Practical enough? Let's say it's the year 1987. Let's say that a few years before you invested your life's savings and watched it boom along with the stock market into a wonderful nest egg allowing you to comfortably retire. Then October 1987 came — October 19, 1987, to be exact. A Monday. What would later be known as *Black Monday*. A day when the stock market would fall 508 points off it's high of 2,246 – the largest single percentage drop of all time. A day when many individual stocks fell to between half and one-quarter of their value.

*Sounds like what happened to my portfolio
in the great NASDAQ slide from 2000 to 2002.*

Yes, but that slide was gradual, not all in one day. And that gave you several options: You could have pulled money out and put it back in at a lower point, or you could have kept your money where it was, maintaining a *vision* of the day the market would inevitably rise again. In that case, your profits would return and probably surpass any previous highs.

But your example shows precisely what *vision* can do for a person:

Vision allows us to look up from the depths of our darkest day and see the light of tomorrow.

OK, so back to the Black Monday scenario.

Right. So let's say, in a single day, you have lost half to three-quarters of your life savings. And let's say something happens at the moment of that downfall that forces you to pull out all your remaining money. You no longer have the option to keep your money in and wait until the market rises again.

Ouch.

And let's say you're not young – you're nearly seventy. You don't have the advantage of decades to make back all you have lost to secure your crucial senior years. How would you react?

Cripes, that would be absolutely devastating!

The above example is from real life. It happened to a former World War II pilot nicknamed *The Death-Cheater*. Yet even at his age, this man began making a great comeback three years later.

The important part of this story is not simply that he came back financially, but he did so by crystallizing 9 universal principles for transforming any low point – any major life challenge – into a pathway of great spiritual and material advancement.

The Death-Cheater had used these same principles as a pilot to escape death during World War II and later taught them to his son.

I am that son.

And you, dear readers, are sons and daughters of that same Vision.

What kind of mumbo-jumbo ... ?

I am the true-life son of *The Death-Cheater*. I decided to share my father's 9 life-changing principles by writing *The 9 Insights of the Wealthy Soul* and, subsequently, the entire *Wealthy Soul* series.

In so doing, my father's Vision became my Vision, and helped others transform and grow according to their own life challenges and receive their own life-sustaining Visions.

While vision with a little "v" allows us to rise from our depths, Vision with a big "V" gives us a grace that brings others up with us.

Hmm. Now, about that NASDAQ tumble from 2000 through 2002 …?

Yes, Al?

I watched my portfolio sink day by day. But I didn't lose hope. I even put more money in when I thought the market was at certain low points. Does that qualify me as a "man of vision?"

Indeed! You demonstrated great vision, Al. However, our entire analogy with the stock market has been about vision with a small "v," which is very different than the *Vision* with a big "V" that we refer to in this book – the Vision that requires a lifetime.

And yet, how you lost money but how you are slowly coming back, illustrates an important principle regarding Vision with a big "V":

Developing Vision provides great tolerance for mistakes. The greater the Vision, the greater the tolerance.

*So, people with Vision – Wealthy Souls *with*
Vision – also make mistakes?*

You bet, Al.

Paradoxically, the greater the Vision, the greater the mistakes!

Huhh? Who wants to make such great mistakes?

Men with Vision take calculated risks. When we're talking about Vision with a big "V" – the Vision and Lasting Purpose of one's lifetime – what gives Wealthy Souls the strength to accept sometimes catastrophic losses is that they do not have a one-month, a one-year or even a ten-year horizon. They have a life-time horizon.

Having a lifetime horizon transforms the meaning of mistakes.

I'll say. Some mistakes can ruin *a lifetime.*

Of course. But they are usually mistakes made out of greed or impatience – not out of being aligned with a Vision.

An ex-president, who perhaps made one of the gravest mistakes in modern history, later commented on how he survived the awesome disgrace and loss of his political life: "It's not over when you lose," he said. "It's over when you quit."

Richard Nixon

After fighting severe depression following his impeachment, Richard Nixon rose from the ashes and came closest to becoming a Wealthy Soul based on the things he did years *after* his presidency ended, rather than from all his achievements *during* it. He wrote books, advised heads-of-state that followed him, and contemplated the bigger picture of not only his life and his mistakes, but how to aid the country and the world with what he had learned and in the way he had been gifted.

Most mistakes are not of the Watergate magnitude. But all mistakes incurred by a Wealthy Soul have certain things in common:

Each is a *lesson* ... an *opportunity* for growth ... not a sign of failure.

Learning from mistakes is a prime means by which the Wealthy Soul advances toward his Vision.

You have used the expression "being aligned with a Vision." *How does a Wealthy Soul know he is aligned?*

He knows by learning not to measure success by any outside standards. Rather, an internal compass tells him when he is on or off course.

The Wealthy Soul's magnetic north is his internal sense of appropriateness.

Explanation, please.

Let me give three examples – two Wealthy Souls who were Heads of State and one who very likely could have been.

The first is ...

Jimmy Carter

As an independent citizen, Jimmy Carter used the skills he had so finely honed as president to quietly advance peace, democracy and health throughout the world. As founder and leader of *The Carter Center*, he has overseen what otherwise might have been fraudulent elections in numerous developing nations. He has negotiated for peace and democracy with intractable dictators. The Center's initiatives combat hunger and disease in Africa, Asia and Latin America. He has written best-selling books about the grace and goodness of life, and — without necessarily using these words – about what makes a Wealthy Soul. And by regularly serving as a high-profile, hands-on volunteer, along with his wife Rosalynn, he helped put *Habitat for Humanity* on the map. This provided exponential growth for the charitable organization, which uses volunteers to build homes alongside the disadvantaged but proud owners who will eventually occupy them.

Someone very profoundly said that Jimmy Carter is the only man who used the presidency as a stepping-stone to his greatest life's work.

What finer tribute can be said?

When a man accomplishes great works __after__ he has achieved the highest success, simply because it is his nature, you are seeing a true Wealthy Soul with true Vision.

*Hmm. Come to think of it, there aren't
many similar examples I can think of.*

Indeed not. But there are Wealthy Souls with many other paths. Which leads to our next example – a man who fought more than a half-century for the Vision he had of his country and his people. He was imprisoned close to 30 years during his struggle. Yet even behind bars, silenced for many years, he became an unconquerable symbol for a nation – and the world.

Nelson Mandela

Nelson Mandela grew up hearing stories around tribal campfires of brave ancestors who roamed the land as free men. The reality of the South Africa in which he was raised was quite different, however. Blacks had no political representation. They were required to carry identification cards allowing their every movement to be tracked, and they were relegated to the life of second-class citizens, often living and working under horrendous conditions.

When he was 26, Mandela joined the African National Congress (ANC) – a political freedom movement – whose ranks he quickly ascended, eventually assuming its leadership.

Arrested in 1956 for ANC activities, he later was released from jail and cleared of the charges. However, he was arrested again in 1962 and would remain a prisoner for the next 28 years.

At age 72, when most men are well into retirement, Nelson Mandela was released from prison to assume leadership of his people, unite his country, and transform the world with the fruition of his life's Vision.

*The power of a
Vision is the
unshakeable faith
in it and its
timelessness.*

I'm not sure I'd want to sacrifice
my retirement working so hard.

Take heart, Al. Sometimes Wealthy Souls distinguish themselves more by what they *don't* do than by what you see them do.
The best example of that is a man who could have been the first
black president of the United States. Instead, this Wealthy Soul
politely turned down offers to run because of inappropriate timing of events with his personal life.

Colin Powell

General Colin Powell was probably the most respected and
trusted person in America after the Gulf War. Yet he was able to
separate himself from ego, opting not to run for the presidency
in 1996. Exemplifying how *special* each Vision is, he cited personal reasons, trusting his own internal compass rather than external forces — which, in this case, provided a temptation that was
historical in nature.

That internal compass – which we all possess but often
choose to ignore – was a product of extraordinary personal
integrity. Among other things, it told Colin Powell that he hadn't
yet – in his own words – "received the *vision* for the country" that
he felt was essential to lead it.

Though four years later he would accept an appointment to
become Secretary of State, in 1996 he recognized that his reser-
vations about the political parties, the scrutiny of the press, the
rigors of a campaign, and a four- to eight-year period when his
life would belong first and foremost to his country rather than to
his loved ones, was not in line with his path at that time.

The highest
calling is heard
not from the roar
of the ego, but
from the whispers
of the soul.

I'm not sure I would have refused an offer to become president.

Each Wealthy Soul has his own path, his own Vision, his own internal compass of appropriateness. No one can know what is right for another, or even fully know what is right for oneself at some future time. All three examples are of similar paths but completely different Visions. Yet all illustrate the same concept of being unbound by external standards or time constraints.

Wealthy Souls march to their own drumbeat.

You have used three famous and powerful men as examples. Do all Wealthy Souls become famous and powerful?

No. Everyone's path is different; some are simple, some are complex. Some lead to notoriety; others lead to simple joy for oneself, one's family, and for those lucky enough to cross paths with the Wealthy Soul.

Any person can become a Wealthy Soul by following a balanced path to a destiny contained within a Vision.

Can you give other examples of Wealthy Souls who followed a Vision?

The mother who dedicates her life to her children, never losing faith, guiding them slowly to fulfill her Vision of them becoming Wealthy Souls themselves.

The doorman who brightens hundreds of people's lives with a smile, kind words and his Vision to see directly into the heart of each person he serves, fulfilling that Vision every hour of every day.

The nurse who sits by the bedside of patients, laughing and crying with them, telling stories, holding hands, whispering words of hope and encouragement to illuminate desperate moments with the Vision of love and things eternal.

The child who gives some of her Christmas or Chanukah gifts to a charity — and later discovers her Vision is to become a mother, a doorman or a nurse like those described above.

There are as many paths and Visions for Wealthy Souls as there are people in the universe.

*God creates every
soul with a
unique path and a
unique Vision for
it to become
wealthy.*

So anyone can become a Wealthy Soul?
Even someone whose career solely involves personal gain?

Absolutely. Lets consider a career as a stock investor. People invest in the stock market to make money. And to be a successful investor, one has to focus on the bottom line.

However, the investor can choose to put his money in potentially high-income companies that he believes will also aid or advance the arts or humanity in some form. Many technology companies fit this description, such as Bill Warner's Avid Technology, or a bio-tech company aiming to crack the DNA sequence to get at the root of certain diseases. Or a natural food-market chain that advocates healthier eating and living. Or an environmental enterprise seeking a more efficient form of energy than gasoline.

This same investor probably wouldn't invest in tobacco stock or a company that caters to totalitarian regimes – even though the company might be extremely profitable.

In the Wealthy Soul's life, the end doesn't justify the means. Rather, the means reflects the Vision.

And what Vision guides a man
whose job primarily centers around profit?

A true Vision provides that each step of the way, personal gain is not sacrificed, but rather *consciously transmuted* into societal good.

The Vision might be to someday – or even more appropriately, *along the way* – help a favorite charitable organization grow its funds by imparting the same knowledge the businessman uses to grow his personal wealth.

Or it could be to become financially secure enough to start a worthy cause himself.

Or it might be to not just provide a smooth path for his children to become Wealthy Souls, but also to mentor other children so that they'll gain the tools, education and encouragement to rise above all odds.

There are few higher callings than to use one's experience to teach another how to be strong, loving independent and giving — how to be Wealthy Souls themselves.

Bernard Dohrmann

Bernard Dohrmann was born into a family of wealth and privilege. His grandfather founded the Emporium Department Store chain across the western United States. Bernard's father, Alan Dohrmann, helped design a human-potential training program that would influence the likes of Walt Disney, Napoleon Hill, Buckminster Fuller and John F. Kennedy.

Born with a winning personality, an uncanny knack for business and a deep sense of people, Bernard Dormund chose a career as an investment banker. He eventually rose to the upper echelons of Wall Street, developing investment companies in 14 countries and transacting billions of dollars in sales.

But on his way to the top, Dohrmann was given a Vision that would change the second half of his life, and that of his wife, Lynn. In 1991, he founded an organization called Income Builders International (IBI). His Vision was to give anyone with a dream the tools to achieve it.

Since 1991, IBI has shown more than 15,000 graduates the principles of the free enterprise system, teaching them how to create a viable business plan, raise the necessary capital, and create the required organization to make those dreams reality. His Free Enterprise Forums also attracts those who've already achieved their dreams – and want to give back as mentors or investors.

Many fine enterprises have been spawned by IBI, the most notable of which is the *Chicken Soup for the Soul* series – among the most successful best-selling series of all time.

But Dohrmann's greatest pride is the teenagers whom he and his mentors have influenced. "When we get adults in our programs," he says, "it's wonderful. They learn how to use the free enterprise system ... training they never had. But a child gets to use this knowledge their entire life ... and it changes their entire world."

Vince Kinsler

At 35 years old, Vince Kinsler was fired from his marketing job at a food services company. With a wife and two little children to support, in his own words, "At that moment, things couldn't have looked bleaker." He moved from a crowded Michigan city to a cozy beachside town in Florida for a higher quality of life for his family.

Then came the challenge of how to earn a living in a town notorious for paying minimum wage. Kinsler realized three things: He no longer wanted to work for someone else, he wanted a business with the potential for high returns, and he wanted to somehow help people in the process. Because he loved children and elderly people, he decided that one of those groups should be in his plans. Because of the large retirement community in his area, he saw huge potential in the home healthcare market.

In 1994 he founded *Affordable Homecare*, which specialized in providing the highest-quality private homecare for ailing seniors. After many years of long hours, financial setbacks, employee heartaches, and pure grit and determination, Kinsler eventually grew Affordable Homecare into an organization of 38 nurses and caregivers that serviced hundreds of elderly patients with the quality of care he envisioned. In the process, he became a wealthy man.

Kinsler now devotes time to lecturing and mentoring teens about obtaining Vision and developing the skills required to turn their Vision into reality. "Because history repeats itself," he says, "and I've lived my share, I feel a strong desire to impart to today's young people the challenges, the blessings, and the wisdom history has taught me. After all, our future is in the hands of those who follow us."

Are Wealthy Souls always strong people?

Wealthy Souls are always people who develop strong spirits, but they don't necessarily have strong bodies.

Oftentimes, illness is the catalyst that makes people look beyond the surface to find true strength and the true wealth of life.

Christopher Reeve

Christopher Reeve might have been just another famous Hollywood actor for his role as Superman. His path was drastically changed when a fall from a horse left him quadriplegic.

Reeve might have given up on life at that point. Rather, he chose to use his fame to help others, subsequently filling his own life with more meaning and purpose than he probably ever would have experienced had he remained just a Hollywood star.

Reeve became spokesman and vice chairman of the board of *The National Organization on Disability*, which promotes the welfare of people with disabilities. He also established *The Christopher Reeve Paralysis Foundation*, which supports research to develop effective treatments and a cure for paralysis caused by spinal cord injury and other central nervous system disorders. The foundation also allocates part of its resources to grants to improve the quality of life for disabled people.

Christopher Reeve became a model for other para- and quadriplegics. He resumed his acting career, starring in a remake of Alfred Hitchcock's movie *Rear Window* and directing *In the Gloaming*, starring Glenn Close, Whoopi Goldberg and Bridget Fonda.

Even after his death, he remains a symbol of hope, of rising above all adversity, and of how ...

Not the body
...rather the
spirit...
can truly learn to
fly.

Jacques Lusseyran

During World War II in France, 16-year-old Jacques Lusseyran became an underground resistance leader of more than a thousand men. He was eventually caught by the Nazis and survived the horrors of Buchenwald concentration camp for sixteen months. Out of the 2,000 men shipped there with him, he was among 30 who survived.

Jacques Lusseyran also was blind. His ability *to see* deep into the souls of men by hearing beyond their words into their hearts gave him the rare ability to weed out spies in his organization. It also gave him an amazing joy of life, which sustained him through the greatest horrors known to mankind. Here was a Wealthy Soul with true *Vision*. In his own words:

"Joy does not come from outside. Whatever happens to us, it is within."

Ryan White

Ryan White probably would have been an ordinary 13 year old except that he had hemophilia, a blood disease that required regular transfusions.

And he might have stayed just another kid who happened to have hemophilia ... until he contracted AIDS from a tainted blood transfusion.

But Ryan still might have lived out his life quite ordinarily until the community he lived in rose up against him and denied him access to school.

Ryan White became *extraordinary* when he decided to take the case to court, fighting not only the ignorance and anger of a school board and an entire town, but that of a nation.

In winning his court case, Ryan White transformed himself into a symbol to the world, showing that AIDS patients need not be treated as ancient lepers, and that the fear of contracting the disease through daily interaction other than through sexual contact, was unfounded.

Ryan became an inspiration for celebrities such as Elizabeth Taylor, Michael Jackson and Elton John. Even more importantly, this unassuming teenager became a symbol for the world – and particularly for those with physical challenges – a symbol of strength, hope and most importantly ... grace under the most extremes of fire.

Through those who physically suffer – much more than through those blessed with health – we see the awesome power of the human spirit to transcend all limitations.

Are there stages to the realization of a Vision?

Yes. The first is obtaining a Vision. It is the most important step.

It may take years – even decades – for a Vision to clarify.

Why so long?

Vision often comes together like pieces of a puzzle. The Wealthy Soul may have an idea of his Vision at a very young age, but until enough pieces of his life come together, he may not be able to see the full picture of how to accomplish it. However, once he does, a *Flexibility of Focus*♦ develops, and progress takes a quantum leap.

♦ See *The Path of the Wealthy Soul,* page 89.

Then all the disparate aspects of life align and the Wealthy Soul becomes like a laser in the hand of The Almighty.

Can you give me an example?

Yes. Something very personal: the evolution of *The Wealthy Soul* series.

I have been writing my entire life. I have also been a professional in the health and wellness field for more than 20 years, during which time I developed various holistic systems and taught many seminars. However, during those years, I often felt there was no true unifying feature to everything I had developed, to the works I'd written and seminars I'd taught. Often it felt as if different aspects of my life conflicted with others. Yet individually, each creation felt truly "received." I led a very happy and materially successful life, but a unifying feature was missing.

Then one day, when I was sitting high atop a rocky plateau in a beautiful Northern Arizona canyon, the beauty of *The Wealthy Soul* concept came to me. I had had the idea for years – since writing my first published book, *Taking Stock*♦. However, it wasn't until that moment, on that mountaintop, that the *primacy* of *The Wealthy Soul* idea materialized. *Taking Stock* was republished as *The 9 Insights of the Wealthy Soul*. And suddenly everything else I'd written and taught up to that point in my life coalesced under one inspiring Vision.

Walter Russell, a famous author, inventor, artist and sculptor of the early 20th century, wrote in his book, *The Genius Inherent in Everyone*:

♦ *Taking Stock* is now available as a collector's item. Visit wealthysoul.com if you want to obtain a copy.

"*Great men's lives
begin at forty.*"

*That's a cause for great hope, especially for those
feeling that life may be passing them by.*

Certainly. Russell, known originally for his presidential paint-
ings and sculptures, produced prodigious works when he was in
his eighties. His volumes of books on universal knowledge were
not completed until after he was age 85.

Once a Vision is clarified – which can occur at *any* age – a
person's true **mission** begins. Taking time and great care to write
a ***mission statement*** is tremendously beneficial in fine-honing
the Vision. From that point forth, the Wealthy Soul has the tools
to operate at peak effectiveness.

The mission statement prevents the Wealthy Soul from heading
off in inappropriate directions, wasting any more time and energy.

The mission statement applies the Law of Conservation of Energy to the Wealthy Soul's Vision.

Wooh, we're getting heavy. Can you explain that?

The Law of Conservation of Energy states that energy cannot be created or destroyed. It can only be converted into other forms.

Likewise, the Wealthy Soul will still live the same life, but everything that comes across his path – and everything important that came out of his path up to that point – will be converted into something useful for the manifestation of his Vision.

Edison

While inventing the light bulb, Edison performed thousands of failed experiments in his attempt to create a long-lasting filament. Then one day he happened to see a button hanging by a thread from his jacket. In a brilliant flash of insight, Edison came up with the idea to carbonize a thread of cotton, through which he would pass a current of electricity. An ordinary sight was converted into a dynamic solution to his Vision, and in so doing, Edison literally illuminated the lives of every generation to come with the first light bulb.

In my own life, when I came up with the mission statement of the *Wealthy Soul* series, I suddenly saw how almost everything I had written, created and taught in the past coalesced under this one idea. Book titles had to be changed, seminars had to be reorganized, and many tweaks to other works had to be made to match the Vision.

BUT ...

*The fit was
– and always had
been – there.*

So what you're saying is, a mission statement gives everything in life new meaning?

Yes. New meaning and *purpose.* It prevents the Wealthy Soul from wasting a lot of time with extraneous things that get him nowhere. It illuminates his path so he doesn't trip in the darkness off the path.

*The mission
statement allows
the Wealthy Soul
to find
The Path of Least
Resistance.*

So what is the mission statement of the Wealthy Soul Series?

Our mission statement is as follows:

To provide a model for transforming our greatest life challenges – and the challenges of those whom we are graced to help – into the highest wealth of the soul.

The Wealthy Soul concept is spiritual in nature. It's easy to see how the mission statement supports a Vision. Can you give an example of a more down-to-earth business with a mission statement that also supports a higher Vision?

Starbucks

Starbucks is one of the first companies I personally ever invested in. My interest originally piqued when I read about the company preparing to open dozens of stores around Atlanta, where I was living at the time. I had been interested in a coffee chain because friends and I had often met at Café Intermezzo, Atlanta's only café in 1994. Café Intermezzo was always packed. My friends and I loved the place even though none of us were coffee drinkers.

Prior to the flurry of coffee chains that followed the advent of Starbucks, bars were the typical meeting place for Americans. Never a drinker, and never having enjoyed being around people who drank, I knew there were plenty of others like me and my friends. The potential of a finely run coffee chain was obvious.

When Starbucks first came to Atlanta, I did a lot of research on the company. The more I researched, the more I liked. Not only was the concept timely, Starbucks seemed to be a company with a conscience. The company supported many environmental and social causes. It provided health insurance to all employees. Employees received extensive education not only on making the finest coffee, but how to share the exotic romance of coffee with their customers. Each store was incredibly well run. And they were all extremely profitable.

My investment in the company turned out to be a prudent one. I profited many times over. More importantly, I learned …

A company founded on a true God-given Vision enriches lives, not simply pocketbooks.

Howard Schultz, Chairman

In his book, *Pour Your Heart Into It*, Howard Schultz, the chairman of Starbucks and the man behind its meteoric rise, described his own path from the slums of New York's Hell's Kitchen. He received the Vision of establishing a chain of European-like cafés that would revolutionize the landscape of the American neighborhood – the exact Vision kindled in me upon seeing my first Starbucks, and the same Vision kindled in the millions of customers Starbucks now serves.

In *Pour Your Heart Into It*, Schultz also shares his company's mission statement. It well illuminates the solid foundation of higher principles from which such a fine company rose. With Starbucks permission, we have reproduced its mission statement here:

Starbucks Mission Statement

Establish Starbucks as the premier purveyor of the finest coffee in the world while maintaining our uncompromising principles as we grow. The following six guiding principles will help us measure the appropriateness of our decisions:

Provide a great work environment and treat each other with respect and dignity.

Embrace diversity as an essential component in the way we do business.

Apply the highest standards of excellence to the purchasing, roasting, and fresh delivery of our coffee.

Develop enthusiastically satisfied customers all the time.

Contribute positively to our communities and our environment.

Recognize that profitability is essential to our future success.

OK, so the mission statement is important.
What's the next important step in realizing a Vision?

The next step is setting **goals**. Goals are like signposts we place in advance along the path we plan to travel so that we keep heading in the right direction. The key to setting goals successfully is to make their timing and their outcome reasonably flexible. It usually takes longer to reach a goal than originally expected, and when you arrive, things may look very different than what you'd imagined.

Goals are the maps of Visions. Don't, however, confuse the map with the territory.

What?

You need a map to cross a desert. But the map doesn't show you every sand dune and cactus. It doesn't show you which tribal wars you'll need to avoid, which sandstorms you'll need to seek shelter from, which oases will charm and delay you while you rest and enjoy your journey.

Goals provide direction. Life provides the path.

*OK. So I have my mission statement. I've set my goals.
Life determines my path. What else is there left
for me to do to accomplish my Vision?*

To work hard. Sometimes very hard. But joyously. And ...

To dream! To dream however extraordinarily your path allows you to. But remember ...

*Set your dreams in
line with your
mission statement,
your goals,
and most
importantly ...
your Vision!*

Can I dream anything?

You can ... that is, once you begin seeking a Vision. Meanwhile, create a mission statement and flexible goals.

For the nuts and bolts tools you'll need to accomplish your goals and realize your Vision, I highly recommend you purchase software for business planning and business organization available at any office supply chain. These programs help you get organized – the first essential step you *must take* to provide the physical foundation on which to build the temple of a beautiful life-supporting Vision.

These tools will help you remain open to modify any aspect of your plan, so that you'll have the flexibility to establish your Vision in all the glorious directions it may take you.

With that foundation, and that flexibility, your dreams will be in line with dreams that will indeed come true. However, without these essentials, you're just daydreaming.

For successful *life dreaming* ...

Don't dream the impossible dream. Dream the probable dream!

 *OK, so my dreams come true. You said earlier a Vision lies* beyond *all dreams. Which leads back to the question I was asking all along …*
What *exactly* is a Vision?

Funny you should ask. A Vision is something *holy*. Many successful men achieve great goals. Some may realize their dreams. But few achieve great Vision. The distinction is that …

Goals are personal.
Vision is immortal.

Which is to say…?

Which is to say that goals can be set. You can sit down with a piece of paper and write goals and mission statements any time to lead to your personal dreams. This is good.

However …

Vision must be received.

Received? As in received from ...

From the Highest. Only by asking, by *praying*, and then by patient waiting ... sometimes for years, sometimes for decades for full illumination ... are we granted true Vision.

Ah, but when we finally receive It! We experience the blessing of one of the most powerful evolutionary events possible for mankind!

In the meantime, don't dally. Write a mission statement. It will clarify with time. Set your goals and invest in the tools to realize them. Then let your dreams guide you.

But *pray* for illumination. *Pray* for Vision.

For Vision is
… exactly …
that which God
sees when looking
through our eyes.

Now that you're done with this Wealthy Soul handbook, it's a good idea to give yourself a break to let its overall message sink in. After a day or so, read the book again very slowly, concept by concept, biographical portrait by portrait, over a period of one to two weeks. Then, each day for the next 6 to 12 months, randomly flip open to any page and see which insight rings true to what you are supposed to be reminded of that day.

Whenever you feel comfortable, begin another *Wealthy Soul* handbook. A number are already written and many more are coming. Each is designed to add concepts that you'll begin to cultivate on your path as a Wealthy Soul.

At some point, you will want to read **The 9 Insights of the Wealthy Soul**, Michael Norwood's personal story and the book that sparked the entire *Wealthy Soul* series. It is a story of a former WWII pilot nicknamed *The Death-Cheater* – Michael's father – who teaches Michael nine universal principles of transforming rocks into diamonds, imminent crashes into soaring flights, and our greatest life challenges into the highest wealth of the soul.

Each subsequent handbook is designed to show a different facet of that rock-turned-diamond so that ...

Any person can transform into a Wealthy Soul — that which we all, on our deepest level, desire to be.

The author in one of his offices.

Michael Norwood is a Doctor of Chiropractic and a board certified kinesiologist and nutritionist with extensive post-graduate training in neurology and holistic medicine. The *Wealthy Soul* series has roots in his childhood, growing up with a sibling who suffered from terminal cancer. The beautiful gifts and grace he received through that experience were crystallized by his father, a former WWII pilot nicknamed *The Death-Cheater*, who taught him *The 9 Insights of the Wealthy Soul* — lessons about transforming adversity into wealth of every kind. His father was battling his own illness at the time.

Michael recently moved to the red rock canyon country of Sedona, Arizona where he teaches seminars and writes *Wealthy Soul* books from various prime office locations.

Skeptic Al . . .
in his new office!

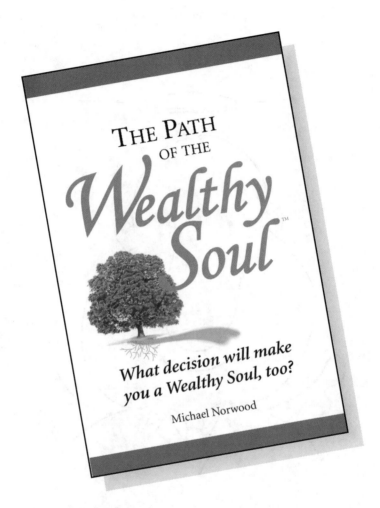

THE PATH
OF THE

Wealthy™

Soul

*What decision will make
you a Wealthy Soul, too?*

Michael Norwood

The unsinkable nature of the human spirit

is the subject of the entire Wealthy Soul series: how to create that spirit, n◦
matter what obstacle, setback, loss, illness or disappointment causes it to
falter. You will learn, just as the models we portray have learned, what
decision transforms all challenges into wealth of every kind!

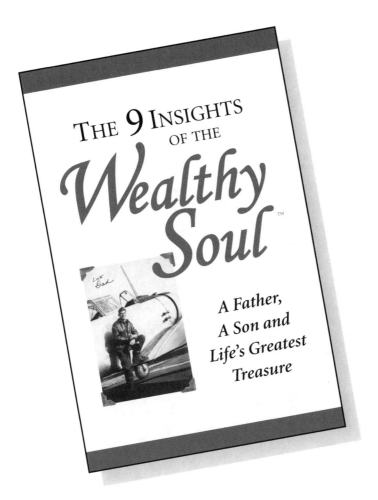

THE **9** INSIGHTS
OF THE
Wealthy
Soul™

A Father,
A Son and
Life's Greatest
Treasure

"Destined to be a classic."
—ROSANNE WELCH
Producer of *Touched by an Angel*

A former WWII pilot — battling a grave illness — teaches his son
9 unforgettable lessons about transforming all our adversities,
setbacks and losses into wealth of every kind.

ORDER FORM

 # Qty:

_____ The 9 Insights of the Wealthy Soul @ $19.95 $_____

_____ The Path of the Wealthy Soul @ $14.95 $_____

_____ The Vision of the Wealthy Soul @ $14.95 $_____

Wealthy Soul Gift Pack (all 3 items above) @ **$29.95** (40% off)

# of Gift Packs:_____ x **$29.95** = $ _____

Subtotal : $_____

SHIPPING & HANDLING:
     U.S.: add $8.95 for 1-3 books,
         and $1 for each additional book. $_____

     Canada: $16.95 for 1-3 books
         $2 for each additional book. $_____

All other countries: $29.95 (Global Express) for 1-3 books
         $3 for each additional book. $_____

     Arizona Residents: add sales tax
         per the county you live in. $_____

TOTAL AMOUNT FOR ORDER $ _____ **.** ____

Telephone Orders: **888-822-4694;** Fax Orders: **206-339-6420**
Web orders: **www.wealthysoul.com**

Mail Orders: Wealthy Soul, 65 Verde Valley School Rd, Suite H13, Sedona, AZ 86351

Name: _____

Address: _____

City:_____ State: _____ Zip: _____

Country:_____ E-mail address: _____

Payment: ☐ Check ☐ VISA ☐ MasterCard ☐ Discover Card ☐ AMEX

Card #:_____ Expires: _____

RECEIVE YOUR *FREE* BONUS GIFTS

at www.wealthysoul.com,
Michael's thanks for having obtained his books:

FREE - Michael's online Wealthy Soul Newsletter. Filled with action steps and stories that will begin transforming all your challenges into wealth of every kind.

FREE inspirational Flash movie presentations of Michael's *30 Gifts of Life* poems. The movies of the poems took Michael 3 years to produce. The links to view them will be emailed to you one per week for 30 weeks. The movies will continually inspire you to discover the greatest wealth in your own life.

FREE audios, radio and television shows, and upcoming teleconferences with Michael. Subjects include Michael's newest revelations about *The 30 Gifts of Life* and *The 9 Insights of the Wealthy Soul.* Continue discovering these exquisite Gifts and Insights everyday on your own path.

Sign up to receive your free gifts at
www.wealthysoul.com